# The Mouse, The Bird, The Dog, and The Lion

## 3 Men to Avoid and 1 to Marry

# Keishorne Scott

# The Mouse, The Bird, The Dog, And The Lion

© 2018 by Keishorne Scott
Requests for information should be addressed
to: **info@keishornescott.com**
Printed in the United States of America
ISBN-13: 9781731023254
Published by Keishorne Scott, Brooklyn, NY

Edited by Yvonne Perry Consulting Services, LLC,
Raleigh, NC

# DEDICATION

*To all the beautiful queens waiting for your king. Be patient; he's on the way.*

# TABLE OF CONTENTS

## THE LION

## CONCLUSION

Mouse
Bird
Dog

# *INTRODUCTION*

D o you think you should respect a man who doesn't respect you when you're not around? Well, if you answered, "Yes," then clearly you have never been with a Mouse Man What about a man who says he's exclusively committed to the relationship but refuses to share passwords to his phone, email, voicemail, and so on? Instead, if you ask him for the passwords, you've just given your Bird Man enough reason to fly the coop. And then there's the man who seems loyal but has a roaming eye for every skirt and booty that passes by. Would you find it hard to trust a Dog Man like him?

Whatever your answer is to any of these scenarios, I want to make something very clear to every woman reading this book. You have the right to be treated like a queen, but some of you reading this aren't treated that way by your man at all. In fact, he tends to have an interesting approach to the whole relationship— he comes half-committed to everything, which means, in 'man talk', he's not interested at all. In the end, he'll either cheat on you, start shopping around for something 'better', or he'll leave altogether.

I think women deserve so much more from men than a lot of us are willing to put in, which brings me to the point of writing this book. My wife Princess and I are raising a beautiful daughter who, we know, deserves a king. Anyway, something disturbing occurred to us. Way too many of our women friends almost always wind up choosing the wrong man to create a future with. We didn't want that to happen to our daughter. When Princess and I discussed the reasons why some of our female friends wind up with losers, we concluded this much from observation.

They simply have trouble picking out the good ones (and, yes, there are still good men out there). Some guys are just good at shrouding themselves in sleekness and all things good—for a while at least. They manage to fool even some of our friends who are highly educated and have good jobs but still wind up with the wrong guy. And for those who manage to find Mr. Right wind up losing him, too, because they didn't know they had to prepare for him (I'll get into that later). Anyway, I wanted to come up with a way to help women understand how to examine men carefully before committing fully. I decided I would compare certain types of men to animals. In all, I came up with three types of men—based on their animal-like behavior—every woman should avoid. The mouse, the bird, and the dog.

Contrarily, there is a type of man I believe every man should aspire to be and a woman would be pleased to have. He's a king in character and a lion by nature.

Finally, to all the men out there who have ever cheated on their woman: there may be a little karma coming your way. I'm telling your secrets. All of them. It's not that I'm a gossip or someone who has a sick fetish to see others destroyed. On the contrary, I'm usually the kind of man to whom anyone can entrust their confidence, and I don't make a life of harboring bad will toward anyone either. But given the recent narratives about men assaulting women in the entertainment industry and elsewhere (and seemingly getting away with it), I felt compelled to publish this book because women—our equals—deserve better. Much better. Right now, my purpose is to help women detect and stay away from fake men. And, for that, I make no apologies.

NO MATTER
HOW GOOD A
WOMAN YOU
ARE, YOU
WILL NEVER
BE GOOD
ENOUGH FOR
A SNEAKY
CHEAT WHO
ISN'T READY
FOR YOU.

# Chapter *1*
## Meet the Mouse Man

D o you know what the number one test is to determine if your man is a cheat? No? Neither did Ellen, an attractive, unassuming woman in search of a soulmate. She wanted things to work out well for her and her partner so much that she failed to ask all the right questions and take note of specific cues until it was too late. From Ellen's story, you'll see that ignorance about men is expensive. It is not cute, considerate, sweet, smart or anything else for a woman not to know what she's fallen in love with and has brought into her space.

Coming from the perspective of a man, it's this simple: if you suspect trust has been breached (even a little), then he's likely a cheat. Read Ellen's story, told to me for this book. And in the event you're tempted to judge her decisions concerning this guy, don't. Ellen's story is nearly every woman's story.

**Ellen's Story**

Wednesday was a nightmare. Mr. James was his usual impossible, insensitive self. Like always, he came up with a lot of extra stuff for me to do without much prep time. Then he has the nerve to expect excellence. It seemed like every call was an irate customer, screaming for their completed tax returns.

After a while, things calmed down a bit and, after putting out fires for Mr. James, I was able to settle back at my desk. It was covered in a rainbow of opened file folders of various colors and sizes, not to mention Post-it notes and messages about missed calls. I rummaged through the messages to see if my boyfriend had called. Nothing. I sifted through them again. Still nothing. I couldn't help thinking, *Well, dang, at least he could've called, especially after fussing at each other like we did last night. I was the one who called the last time and the time before that. Why can't he call for a change?*

Then it hit me. For the past two months, he had become evasive, withdrawn, and more active at night. I wondered what was keeping him out so late, so I asked him.

"We got a new contract, and I've been selected as the project manager over it. I'm going to be late a lot. I meant to tell you. Guess it slipped my mind. Sorry, bae."

He also said he needed the money. To tell you the truth, we both needed money. Still, I would beg him to try to stick around more, you know? I missed him. Even though he said he'd try, he continued to come home well into the night.

It got to a point where there was hardly anything I could do to change things between us. It was like he was drifting away from me. Still, I tried. Like a couple of nights ago, I fixed his favorite meal—stuffed pork chops with green beans sprinkled with candied pecans and loaded baked potato on the side. The whole dinner was going to be a surprise. I thought it would be nice to spice the evening up by surprising him when he came home. Plus, it was Friday, and I wanted to start the weekend with some fun. I did everything to get his attention.

I set the table in my good silverware, stem glasses and the china that Momma passed on to me. Afterward, I changed into the dark blue dress that he liked so much. He said it set off my brown eyes. Once everything was ready, I sat down in the living room and waited to hear his footsteps. Except all I heard was the ticking of my wristwatch in the silence while the second and minute hands moved purposefully from 5:00 p.m. to 5:30 p.m., 6:15 p.m. and then 7:00 p.m. I looked over at my phone expecting to see a missed call or a text. A blank screen looked right back at me. I don't like being one of those women who's always calling her man checking on him. I wanted to give him space to call me, which is why I spent a few moments in deep thought weighing the pros and cons of calling him.

Finally, I couldn't stand the wait anymore. I picked up my cell phone and began to call him. I couldn't help giggling to myself as I thought about how I would tell him that I couldn't wait to see him and about the surprise I had waiting for him at home. He picked up on the first ring. Before I could even get, "Hello," out, he immediately informed me [brusquely] that he was in a meeting and would call me back. Then click! It took him precisely two seconds to shatter my excitement!

I slumped back into the sofa and drifted to sleep as the hour ticked away to 8:30 p.m. At 11:55 p.m., I awoke out of my sleep to hear the jingling of keys opening the door. *Finally!* I thought. As he walked in he noticed my beautifully set table, looked at me in my blue dress then mumbled an apology. I was livid! It wasn't like I had a lot of time on my hands to cook, was less busy than him or needed to fill space with activity. No. I just thought it would be nice to spend Friday evening together and start the weekend with something fun. I told him this much, thinking he'd understand. Instead, we wound up yelling at each other for an hour about that night and everything else before turning in.

For the rest of the weekend, we hardly said a word to each other, and now it was a new week, and I was back at the grind. I sat at my desk wondering what was going wrong with the whole relationship. In the distance, I heard Mr. James' loud footsteps coming up the aisle toward my cubicle. Out of reflex, I nervously dropped my phone, thinking he was on his way to my cubicle. Instead, he rounded the corner to see another co-worker.

What a relief because the office was a madhouse, and I didn't need another thing to do. Six people didn't come in because of the flu. Those who did show up wanted me to do everything for them— call this person, email that person, attend this meeting, go here, go there, fetch this, fetch that.

Hours later, it was time to leave, and I was thankful to go home and relax. *Maybe he'll be there,* I'm thinking, *fixing dinner for us.*

No such luck. He didn't come home early, nor did he call. So, I spent the evening staying up late preparing financial reports for my boss. After a while, I turned on the late-night news. Immediately I wished I hadn't. Each station was reporting the same tragic event—a local drive-by shooting near his office building.

My mind automatically shifted from the financial report to him. I couldn't keep up the writing after that news report. Anxiously, I got up from my seat and started pacing, praying he would get home safely. Not long after, I heard the engine to his Camaro pulling into the garage. When I met him at the door, I noticed how tousled his hair looked. In fact, his whole outfit seemed equally unkempt. It's funny. I stood there a second trying to recall the last time this usually neatly-dressed, good-looking man ever looked so out of place. Nothing came to mind because, as long as I've known him, he's never looked like that except when he's getting ready to work out.

"I'm home. I missed you all day," he managed to say, walking past me without a kiss hello.

"I missed you too. What took you so long? How come you didn't call? I was worried about you. Did you know there was a drive-by shooting near your office?"

He turned around and looked at me with a blank stare. I could tell he knew nothing about it—even with all that commotion that happened right outside his office. He started to explain how some foreign investors kept him late. *Okay,* I thought, but that didn't solve the disheveled hair or the wrinkled dress shirt and pants. If I didn't know better, I'd have sworn he'd been wrestling.

I wanted to trap him with a question about why he didn't seem to know about the drive-by shooting but decided to let it go—for the time being. "Dinner's warming in the oven if you want it."

He replied, "I'm good."

After worrying about this man, that's all I got— "I'm good." No hint of appreciation for the worrying or anything. Just, "I'm good."

He didn't even notice me staring at him as he laid down on the couch, feet up and cell phone in hand, texting away. Every text he received in response brought on a grin. Even if he sensed I was staring at him, he didn't try to suppress the smiles.

I leaned in closer to the couch and asked, "How's that project going?"

"Fine," he replied without looking up or putting his phone down.

"So, what exactly are you working on again?"

"It is too technical for you to understand, Ellen." With that, he pulled himself up from the couch, cupped his phone in his hand and headed to the bathroom to shower.

About a half hour after we settled into bed, his phone rang. He bolted out of bed in no time and snatched it up from the dresser.

"I can't hear you that well. Bad signal," he tells the caller while looking back at me. "Let me move to where I can hear you." He kept the phone close to his ear as he walked out of the bedroom down the hall, leaving me with a string of questions. *Is he cheating on me? Why don't I trust him? What is he hiding? Why is he hiding?*

## My Answer to Ellen

This ends the story of Ellen's suspicions about her boyfriend, who she thought was "the one". After she shared these incidences with me, she asked, "So, what do you think is going on, Keishorne?"

I broke it to her as gently as I'm breaking it to you: "I'm sorry to break this to you, but your partner is nothing but a Mouse Man," nodding my head up and down as I told her. "Yep. You've been sleeping with a mouse."

# *Chapter 2*
## **Recognizing the Mouse Man**

That frown you have on your face right now from reading Chapter One—it's the same expression my friend had on hers when she finally realized she had been dating the Mouse Man.

You may be asking, "The Mouse Man? Who is he?" Well, let me begin by saying this: a man might be mousey for several reasons. It is not always the case that he's cheating on you. For instance, he might be engaging in activities or friendships that you don't approve of, but that doesn't make him the Mouse Man. However, you will know if your man is the Mouse Man if and when he starts exhibiting the following traits. He comes off as shy, but a careful watch on his behaviors indicates he's just a sneaky rascal. Nearly everything he does is shrouded in secrecy, that's why getting details out of him is like pulling teeth. He'll shut you out of things in a heartbeat. Communication and sharing everyday matters? That's just not his thing.

Here's something else. A mouse is a master at hiding. He will burrow holes into a wall to protect himself from capture and scoot into any of them to get away from you. As masterful as he is at burrowing holes, his carpentry work is shallow at best. They are easy to find, which means he will be too. Anyway, the Mouse Man does not like being seen and would do anything to make sure his activities are hidden. Hence, the sneaking around, just like a mouse in the dead of night does as he creeps along the baseboard in your home so that you don't see him, catch him, and get rid of him. Of course, your mouse partner is human and is too tall, too big and too broad actually to fit into a hole. Nonetheless, he can exhibit mouse ways over and over. Here's one way; like a real-life mouse, your mouse man goes to great lengths to shield/hide his actions. For instance, he'll put a password on his cell phone, tell you what it is, then change it again without telling you. You may wonder why give you the password if he's going to change it? From what I've observed from my gender, I find that the Mouse Man is a deceiver, which makes him untrustworthy. He will lure you into trusting him, only to break your heart with lies and deceit. Remember all the sneaking around he does? Well, that's deception. A real man (whom you'll meet later on in this book) would merely tell you where he's going, do what he has to do when he's gone, then return when finished.

Your partner may also exhibit a mousey trait by hiding specific conversations from you. Remember how my friend's mouse man retreated to other parts of the house to conduct conversations on his phone? Now, I'm the first to admit we all want privacy and it's needed in some cases. But when your partner has to sneak off into a corner or anywhere else in the house to hide his conversations from you, I would think there's a problem, especially when he's taken dozens of other calls from siblings, cousins, his close friends, and even his momma right in your presence. He saw no need to sneak away and talk then. The point I'm making is this: do not fall for the deception. You're so much wiser than that.

The Mouse Man is also skilled at cover-ups. If you are looking to find Stacy, Kimberly, and Hannah in his phone, you will be disappointed.

Since he is good at covering up, Mouse Man will not save the name of other women in ways that will make you suspect him. For example, Kimberly could be KM Consulting. Hannah could be Hank's Barber Shop. Just like a mouse, he is very good at trying not to get caught. He might even have a second phone— one that he hardly ever brings out. Lately, you also notice that he has been more outgoing. A man who generally only goes out once a week now decides that stepping out three or four times a week—without you—makes him come alive.

On some occasions, you have offered to bring him dinner at work, but he declined every time. If this has been the case, the Mouse Man is just living his nature. He doesn't take the dinners because there are times when he leaves work early to have dinner with another, though he returns home well after hours to you. Not that I am trying to build a sense of paranoia in anyone, surely people leave work early and come back late for all kinds of reasons. It's just that in the case of disloyal partners, there is a pattern where they tend to leave the house early just in time to see someone else.

What about business trips? Let's say he told you he's going on a business trip but forgot that he slipped up two months ago when he mentioned that his company had cut their travel budget. A two-day business trip now starts on Friday and spans the entire weekend because Mr. Mousy has to settle in, prepare his pitch, and review his notes so that he can nail the presentation at noon on Monday. In the event, you ask to go along. Forget it. Expect the Mouse Man to give the excuse that you have a job to attend to as the reason for not bringing you along. In response, you tell him that you can take Friday off. He counters by saying that his company's policy prohibits guests, including family, to accompany employees on business trips, something to do with them being a possible distraction. No doubt this inaccurate information leaves you confused at how going on a weekend trip with him can be against company policy.

When it comes to events sponsored by your family, he cites being interrogated by them as a reason for sitting out dinners or not spending holidays with them. But when you tell him that you are opting out of the event to stay with him, he protests and finds any excuse for you not to stay. By the way, when it comes to his family, he's all for going to the outings—but not with you. So, he'll conjure up an excuse to have you stay home or go elsewhere to have fun. Again, the whole point is to sneak in some fun with someone else.

You can also spot the Mouse Man by monitoring his nightly movements. Think about this: a mouse's favorite time of the day isn't when it is sunny and bright. The risks of getting caught are higher during that period. Daytime gigs are not his thing for the same reasons robbers prefer the camouflage of the night. Yes, indeed, night-time is the optimum time to scurry about in secrecy to sneak food away into his burrow. Similarly, the Mouse Man prefers doing his dirt in the dark. What I mean by this is that his sneaky activities happen out of your sight, which is why he'd prefer you not do something like walk into his workplace unannounced. Anything could happen, like you walking up on him while he's flirting with one of his sexy co-workers.

Mice are nocturnal critters, which means their senses are heightened in the dark. With adversity toward daylight, they forage in the night for food and … mates. Here's how that applies to the Mouse Man. Let's say that you two spend an evening together at a club. Instead of focusing only on you, his eyes will dart back and forth scoping out other women in the barely lit club to approach later when he's not around you.

The mouse always leaves a trail. One of the signs that your home is infested with mice is that you will often find chewed up wire, papers, magazines, and insulation, etc. in the house. With the mouse leaving a trail, it's not hard to track his activities. In the case of the sneaky Mouse Man, his trail to other women is filled with paper and wrappers, too, like receipts from hotel stays and restaurants, dinners out, theater or Broadway tickets, condom wrappers and so on. However, he will not want you to see certain expenditures and phone numbers, so he might keep them at his office. He might even rent a mailbox for bills, new credit cards or private letters. Of course, he won't tell you about any of this. He's the Mouse Man, after all, and a genius at hiding. But like any human being, he will eventually make a mistake.

Sometimes, God will shine on you. He might forget a receipt in the pocket to his jacket or bag; or if he doesn't, you might, by sheer luck, come across the Post Office box key on his keychain. Mind you, he may have a good reason for having a separate mailbox address. People who move a lot use them. But think about this: you two have been together in the same place for some time. Therefore, if you are the type who searches well, you will be surprised to find that he has a secret box.

With deception being key in how the Mouse Man deals with his relationships, it may not be surprising that he has issues with honesty. He is neither here nor there. For this particular reason, you may tend to worry21a lot about what he's feeling and thinking. If he says he is at the art gallery, you can't be sure whether he is enjoying exploring the artistic beauty because he really likes art or if he's there to scope out other women. So, you worry about his whereabouts. Then, for all you know, your Mouse Man could be at a fancy restaurant enjoying the beauty of a mystery lady who also happens to appreciate art or is an artist herself.

When he says, "Baby, we can't afford this," what he means is, "I do not want to spend my money on you." You may initially want to believe him, but you aren't sure he is telling the truth because you see him wearing a $4000 wristwatch and fancy, expensive clothing, even though he has been telling you that his sister or some other close relative bought those items because they want him to look good to make a good impression at his workplace. After all, he reasons, research suggests wearing the right outfits and having a particular look captures the boss's attention and may lead to promotion in upper management.

## Reasons for the Mouse Man'! Disloyalty, and Inability to Tr

I want to end this chapter on ᵗʰᵉ ˢ by explaining a couple of reasons for his mousiness. First, when it comes to establishing a new relationship with someone, all the secrecy might be because he is still adjusting to you. It could be that your Mouse Man naturally has difficulty trusting others because of some traumatic experience he endured long before he ever met you. Out of a need to protect himself, he discovered that sneaky and deceptive—even disloyal—is the thing to be to ensure he doesn't get hurt again.

Therefore, he may not be so willing to share his activities with you if he has had a bad experience in past relationships. In this case, it will be better to have an honest conversation with him concerning your feelings and expectations. My opinion, though, is that because the Mouse Man generally has issues with trust, honesty, and loyalty because of a negative experience, opening up to

..an about his secrecy is problematic for him. ..at experience cuts him to the core and healing from it has not happened. For this reason, I caution you to bypass any man you suspect to be the Mouse Man. You cannot heal him, only he can do that, and if he hasn't done so before he met you, it won't happen when he's with you.

Our man might also hide stuff from you if he thinks you can't handle the truth. For example, if he likes to be around women, he might think it best to hide this from you. Some men still have this notion that women are generally clingy and jealous and that it is better to keep them in the dark when it comes to certain things—like hanging out with other women. You should, however, understand that wanting to befriend other ladies doesn't automatically translate into cheating.

However, in some cases, these feelings turn out to be true. Now, the Mouse Man is a master at evasion; you may try to run to keep up, but he's always one step ahead. Like a mouse, he moves very quickly. Therefore, chasing after him might be an ineffective option because you will exhaust your time, energy, and emotions.

Regardless of whatever reasons the Mouse  Man is mousy, secretive behaviors erode trust. And the foundation of a good relationship is trust. If you are in a relationship with the Mouse Man, then trust is lacking because the secrecy and deception cannot undergird a healthy relationship in any way whatsoever. If you want your relationship to move forward, you both need to discuss how to deal with these problems of trust, secrecy, lack of loyalty to you or the issues I laid out earlier and the best way to communicate.

# Chapter *3*
## Trapping the Mouse Man

Not that I advocate dating or marrying a mouse man, but I understand that some women just need evidence to 'catch him in the act' of lying, deceiving, cheating, and anything else he does to continue the secrecy. So, to help them out, I have developed some strategies that can be put into play quickly with little trouble. Remember, there's a trap for every mouse.

## Be spontaneous

Occasionally show up—unannounced—at his gym, workplace, or his favorite hangout spot. If you're not living together, visit his apartment at times when he least expects you. Be ready with a reason for the surprise visit, such as your route is close to his place, so you thought you would visit. If he has nothing to hide, he will welcome you with a broad smile. If he does, he will be extremely surprised or even angry with you for the unannounced visit. You know how mice scurry into hiding when you turn on the kitchen lights? That's how he'll be. He may even rush to hide something from you immediately before you enter.

Mice love trash. So, while you are at his apartment, check the recycle bin for another person's photo, a bill, a note, etc. Do the same with his email (if you have access to it) and ferret out the recycle bin, which people neglect to empty. In either case, there is always a chance of discovering a snippet of information that could be useful later when you confront him about all the deception.

## Be on the alert

Mice are generally fast and skilled at avoiding people. Still, they almost always leave something behind that makes you aware of their presence. For instance, you will know a mice-infested cupboard or building because of the dead giveaway, the distinct ammonia-like smell of their urine or feces.

In the case of the Mouse Man, you may notice that he has started using a more seductive, intense cologne that he never used before and that you did not buy. Has he been working out more lately? Is he wearing more jewelry now than he used to? Does he keep cologne or hairspray in his car? Is he the kind who usually pays little attention to his outfit but is now sporting manicured nails? What is motivating these extra efforts to look fine and smell good? Maybe a new woman in his life? Do not keep guessing. Just ask him outright. If he is evasive, then there is your answer.

## 4 Use keylogger and spyware

If it ever gets to a point where you cannot trust him anymore, and you need to know for sure whether he is up to something or not, you can install keylogger on his computer. Be advised that this is unethical. For a small fee, you can download keylogger on his PC. The program will record whatever it is you want and relay whatever it finds to you over the internet: passwords, pages visited, screenshots of activities.

On his phone, dial *#06# to get his IMEI number. You will need this to install the spyware, which you can then use to monitor his movements, his emails, and even texts. Many spyware applications can be bought legally online, but it pays for you to know the legal implications of using them in your state before you start. Also, be careful not to get addicted to the point where you can't do anything else but watch his every movement. And truth is, if you really feel like you cannot trust him anymore. Leave! You don't have to do any of the things listed above, especially the keylogger. If you feel as if trust is being breached often, and you're sick and tired of it. Just walk away. You deserve better!

## Change your sleeping habits

Mice are nocturnal creatures. Similarly, the Mouse Man may stay up late with the excuse of having to work late. He may change his sleeping habits overnight, and this is what you will also do if he does. He may even take more bathroom breaks than necessary. When you see these changes, take note of when he leaves the bed for a long time, perhaps to receive a phone call.

As appealing as committing his sleek activities to the night may be, do not think about late nights only. The Mouse Man may wake up early before the break of dawn to talk to another woman, especially if he finds that you are beginning to get suspicious. Al-ways be one step ahead.

## Follow up after a fight

Many cheating Mouse Men often use conflicts to camouflage their true intentions. They tend to slam the door after a small disagreement and run into the arms of the other woman; this makes for a great cover. If your mouse man has been slamming doors lately, take the initiative to follow up and see where he is going. Chances are he may be going to see his mystery mistress. Be sure to make yourself as undiscoverable as possible. If he finds out that you are following him, say you wanted to apologize. But if you don't get caught, then you might be on the verge of discovering something great.

In conclusion, you will need a lot of patience to catch the Mouse Man. Don't jump to assumptions too early. Yes, he may be shady and secretive, but that doesn't mean he is cheating on you. Don't jeopardize what may be a good relationship over fears that are unfounded, so it might be a good idea to try some of these traps

I mentioned. Confront your Mouse Man with all your observations. You don't want to throw away a good relationship on assumptions. They say women have a sixth sense for detecting if a man is lying or not. Let God and your sixth sense guide you. Look out for discrepancies in explanations and point them out. If he wants to show you that he cares, he will be transparent and allay your fears. Give him a chance to explain. But if he is acting like he doesn't care about your emotions and you can see that many of the actions of the Mouse Man explained here prove to be true, trust your intuition and look for hard evidence. It is better to confront your fears than to stub-bornly ignore the red flags.

*Keishorne Scott*

# SOME MEN ARE LIKE BIRDS... THEY FLY HERE AND THERE.

## Chapter *4*
## **When the Bird Man Flies**

In May 2011, a famous bodybuilder, award-winning actor, and former government official came under the ax for cheating on his wife of 25 years, who was a prominent television journalist. Since infidelity happens all the time in Hollywood and amongst politicians, that wasn't news to a lot of us. The former politician had a child more than fourteen years earlier with an employee in their household. In my opinion, this guy was just a bird man. Read the following story to see if you happen to have the Bird Man as your lover.

Perhaps you and your man did not have the time to enjoy each other's company. So, one day, you called him to discuss coming to his home for a brief visit. He said, "Sure," and you immediately packed your bags, full of expectations for a great weekend, though your plane was not due to depart for another three days. The day of the trip came, and you took the first flight out of your location. It took a few hours before you arrived at your destination. From the airport, you had to take a taxi and ride two hours before you arrived at his place. It was lovely seeing him standing on the front porch with his astonishing smile. A few hours after you arrived, your conversation took a dark turn. For some reason you can't remember, he brought up an issue from the past about how you never seem to want to move where he is. You responded by reminding him that moving now would cost you seniority at your job and other financial consequences. At that, he fired back accusing you of being selfish by not doing what he wants. He then picked up his phone, made a quick phone call, grabbed a jacket and stormed out of the house. You had planned to spend quality time together; but with him gone, you don't know what to do. Plus, that isn't your house.

It was then reality hit you like a ton of bricks. With the slightest provocation and boredom, he always found a way to just up and leave, give up on the relationship for a while, then come back, only to leave again, and sometimes he left for days. Do you want to know the truth? Like Schwarzenegger, he is probably a Bird Man.

## The Bird and the Bird Man

A bird rarely stays in a place for long even if it has a nest. Before returning to its nest, it will fly from one tree to the next and from one flower to another, sucking nectar until it's full. Now, there are different kinds of birds out there—some who make their nests and some who don't. In this chapter, we will be talking about those who do.

Birds fly for many reasons. They use flight as a means of escaping predators. They fly to get an aerial advantage when sourcing food and hunting down prey. They use flight to improve their and their offsprings' chances of survival by migrating to a different region. When birds migrate, they do so from areas of low or decreasing resources to areas of high or increasing resources, such as food and prime nesting locations.

As birds migrate to fulfill their needs and increase their rate of survival, so do men. Men will migrate from a relationship with one woman to another and on to another for many reasons. One reason has to do with his needs; when they are not being met, the Bird Man will take flight from nesting with one woman to another. You should know that the Bird Man is a master at flying. He has developed structures, behaviors, and habits over the years to help him perfect his art. He loves his freedom and will do anything to keep it.

While the needs of any one man are vast and even vary from another's, some needs run universal across men. For example, every man wants financial stability and physical security. Ladies, call me a chauvinist, but I do not believe it is your responsibility, your duty or your obligation to provide either of these if you are not married to the man. No husband benefits until you say, "I do." A Bird Man will likely disagree. Why? Because he flies from woman to woman looking for these very securities to be provided by another, not himself. Think about it; if he's not providing well for himself, what makes you think he will provide well for you? Based on some men who I have seen mistreat women—the answer is he won't. So, stop wishing, stop fussing and stop hoping for change because it's not going to happen. Besides, no queen-conscious woman wants an undeserving bird pecking at her goods with no means of contributing to the 'kingdom'.

But there are many needs beyond economic and physical security that a man might need.

There's sex and having someplace to stay. If a Bird Man finds that a woman is unable to provide these other needs, this might prompt him to fly from that nesting place to another in search of fulfilling his needs. Again, there's nothing wrong with having needs. We all have them. If I take care of my lady's needs, she sees to mine. The trouble is, ladies, if you make it your business to grant a guy husband benefits (sex before marriage, paying for dinner out, preparing dinner in, cleaning up after him, and so on), there is no guarantee that this man will put a ring on it. In fact, you may be auditioning for a role you may never win.

Here's another factor about Bird Men to keep in mind. In many cases, when flying away to nest with another woman, the Bird Man might just be looking to build another nest where he can get all the comfort that he desires, including peace and little discord. There, in his new cozy nest, he will take and take and take. I have seen men do this over and over again, so has my editor. She told me about one of her older sisters falling prey to the Bird Man. Things started out nice enough—years ago. Then, over time, Bird Man began nesting her out of her house and home. My editor tells me her sister did everything to take care of his needs. After a while, she got nothing in return—except for a broken heart. All those wife privileges went down the drain, and Bird Man, of course, found a new tree to nest in.

Bird Men are not only poor creatures who do not give back, but they also tend to lack vision, which is why they are so unstable and actively flighty. Unlike other men, they have not "written the vision and made it plain". That is, if you ask the Bird Man what he will be doing five years from now, he will stutter at a concrete answer. Long-term planning for him is out. And here's something else, based on some stories another woman told me about past relationships, it doesn't sound like the Bird Man can handle stress. When stress becomes too much for him to bear and an opportunity arises for him to leave the cage that he has found himself in, he might not have to overthink before he takes the opportunity to fly away to a nest where he can live in the moment and forget about his problems and sorrows.

## Some Things to Consider If You Want the Bird Man to Stay

No matter how I have characterized the Bird Man, there will be some women who will want to keep him anyway. If you're one of them, here are some things you'll need to keep in mind as you try to convince him that you're the one he's been looking for all along.

First, like anyone else, the Bird Man wants to be understood. This is one of his desires, in fact, to be emotionally connected. There's nothing wrong with that so long as he has verbal skills to express his emotions well. Most men do not, and so they tend to shut down quickly and become less vocal in some cases when you need them to speak up. This is probably the last thing you need him to do when the two of you are arguing. You may want him to express his feelings about an issue. However, if he doesn't, you become irritated with him and begin provoking him to talk. Now, this may prove to be a fatal move for the relationship because the more you provoke the more your Bird Man will strongly consider flying away.

You would think a pat on the back when things are going rough is welcome by anyone. Well, the truth is a lot of men don't consider it a manly thing to ask for a pat on the back when things are rough. Yet, they need it and desire it. Because they do not voice this desire, their women may tend to overlook their feelings and carry on as usual; this is why it is crucial that you develop and foster a culture of appreciation and thoughtfulness in your relationship. Once you set the tone, he may rise and match it. Of course, it is not always easy and, in fact, could be ter-rifying. First of all, you might have your issues and battles that you are fighting. You have your work, you have a brother or sister to take care of after work, your kids are calling for constant attention, everything around you is demanding attention—and now your man? Instead of merely placing all of his emotional baggage onto you, he should also be helping you. But on the other hand, this is not typical behavior of Bird Men. As I stipulated earlier, stress equals time to fly.

You have to realize that you both have equal responsibilities when it comes to carrying emotional baggage. If he listens to you as you complain about your bad hair day, the kitchen, and the credit you aren't getting at work, he deserves a listening ear too. Real intimacy involves sharing a lot of details and being able to create room for the other person, even if you are overwhelmed with your problems already. The same is tricky for the Bird Man. If you do not take away his issues, he will take flight because the stress is too much for him, even stresses you did not cause. Yes, the Bird Man will fly away to another woman's nest and she will solve his troubles.

Secondly, when it comes to sex, the Bird Man can be flighty. With a concentration on his own sexual needs, he feels he must seek out the one (or ones) who will satisfy him accordingly. Not that this is a defense or excuse, but, biologically speaking, we men need sex. Yes. I said, "need sex." Whether we are married, separated, divorced, single or widowed, our minds can easily drift to sex. I'm making a point of this because sex is often the leading cause of migration for the Bird Man. While birds are socially monogamous, the same is not true for the Bird Man as described in this book. In the case of your sex life, if it hasn't been great lately and he is bored of routine, he will fly. That's his nature. Do not look for him to be any different. Loyalty is just not a part of his character. So, keep that in mind when you decide to try to hang on to the Bird Man.

Now, before you blame yourself in any way for having a sexual relationship with the Bird Man, I want you to remember what you are dealing with. You are dealing with a man who will take flight for just about any reason. Though I may have given you an idea of what to expect if you decide to keep a Bird Man around, I would rather you do as I would tell my daughter if she ever thinks she wants such a man. Kick him to the curb. There are better men who will appreciate you. That is a not a cliché. It is the truth.

# *Chapter 5*
## Keeping the Bird Man

### The Nature of Freedom and the Bird Man

I believe it's instinctive, natural even, for all of God's creatures to want to be free. Therefore, the freedom to move anywhere, feed anywhere, and do as one pleases is something birds want too.

When it comes to freedom in a relationship, some men are like birds. They want to be the typical freedom-lover so that they can take flight when it pleases them. Of all the men I have observed in my lifetime, this is a trait that cuts across different types of men that include the Mouse Man, the Bird Man, or the Dog Man (more on him later). Men from each of these types want to be able to do certain things at will—even though they may be in a relationship with a woman. For example, they may want to go out with the guys whenever and forever long they want, receive calls from other women and have long chats with them, smile endlessly at a Facebook message from another lady without being accused of having an affair with her. They will even take long walks (without their partner)—all without being questioned by the one they're supposed to be committed to. But the realities of life and human nature make this problematic for men who are with women. It could be a bit difficult to maintain a balance between being committed to someone and still being able to do what you like. The design of relationships and marriage doesn't permit a lot of freedom, and every decent man should know this. But the commitment to a relationship is not for everybody.

A real, serious man should know that being answerable to his significant other comes with the territory of being in a relationship, and that goes both ways. A real man should understand that taking flight doesn't solve any issue. It merely postpones friction and judgment day. Flying away from a disagreement instead of staying to communicate and seek a resolution will create harmful consequences that, when put off for the time being, will only heighten their impact in the future.

**True Freedom**

Every man should know that flight does not equate to freedom. True freedom results from the decisions he makes with his partner after they have discussed the matter. Real freedom is what he can achieve when he builds a relationship on a foundation of trust. Real freedom is when his partner

can confidently vouch for him and say to anybody inquiring about his whereabouts, "Oh, you
will find him at such-n-such between the hours
of 2 and 4 PM. If you don't, he is either at Pete's
place with the guys or here with me at the house."
Real freedom is his partner being able to trust the
words that flow from his mouth.

So, now that I've told you what real freedom
is, let me share what it is not. Real freedom is
not deception of any degree, at any time. Ladies,
this is something the Bird Man does not understand. Real freedom is not telling you that he is
going to the gym to play basketball, for example, and then screaming inside *Hurray!* because
you believed him—again. I don't think I need to
tell you where your Bird Man was headed, do I?
With that said, let's consider what true freedom
is. Pure and simple, it is being realistic with yourself. For instance, how can anyone say he or she
is with someone else (in a relationship) and still
act single? So, when it comes to a Bird Man, my
question is, "Why wouldn't you expect her to be

jealous when you spend a significant amount of time on the phone with another woman whom she doesn't even know?"

## How to Keep the Bird Man (if you must)

I have said this before, and I'll repeat it. When someone is beneath you—get rid of him. Don't waste your time. He's not worth it, and you're better than that. And, as hard as I preached about dumping the Bird Man in the chapter prior, there are still some women out there who will disregard my advice and insist on keeping him around, no matter what. So, for you women, I included this chapter— against my editor's advice, I might add— with suggestions on how to keep that flighty rascal in place. And, let me add this disclaimer: following these suggestions is not a guarantee that he will remain with you. He's a Bird Man, for gosh sakes!

Many reasons prompt the Bird Man to fly away from a woman. Bickering and nagging are at the top of his list. They both spell trouble for him, and when there is trouble in the nest, the Bird Man flies away to nest somewhere else. Generally speaking, flying off to another nest to get away from a problem solves nothing. And, while going out to walk off an argument might appear helpful, it may not help that much because it only postpones the fight for another day. So, here is what you could do: make a pact with him that when there is an argument, you each get to walk off the steam to place sometime (i.e., an agreed upon amount of time) and space between you. Then, once the time limit has been reached, you both come together and discuss the issue at hand. The goal is to address the problem, not how Bird Man took flight and returned late, making you angrier than before.

Don't go beyond the scope of the issue by adding that he never helps with anything. While he may not be helping you out with toilet protocol and doing some chores, he may be doing other things like paying some of the bills, cooking the meals, securing the house, doing the plumbing, and many other things that make your life easy. If you are not specific about your complaints, he may not know where to begin. Instead, he may perceive you as quarrelsome, which, in turn, tempts him to fly into the arms of another woman. Keep the argument constructive, which raises another suggestion for keeping Bird Man around.

Watch what you communicate and how. Sometimes, the magic in getting people to do what you want is not what you say but how you say it.

Don't push your Bird Man away by your words and actions. Even though men act tough, there is only so much a man can take when he is frustrated and pushed to the wall. The Bible states, "Kind words turn away wrath."

The key to weathering any stormy relationship is having the mindset to stay together through it all—the good and bad. When anyone goes into a commitment with the mentality that he or she can always find relief in the arms of another person, the relationship is already doomed. People are usually able to find solutions to their problems when they have no other alternative but to face them head-on. As a matter of consequence, that's when they begin to look inwards to identify the source of their problems and effective solutions.

We need to understand that having open, honest communication also works with discussions around money, which remains a slippery slope in just about every relationship. Now, let's be clear about something, ladies. A broke man is never able to provide for his needs, much less yours. Over time his negative bank account balance might start to take a toll on the relationship. And it is in the nature of many women not to take kindly to being with a broke man. If your Bird Man is broke or going broke, I suggest you have this open communication with him. "If you do not get a job or better-paying position in three or four months, then you can just take the next flight to another chick because your time with me will be over." Then keep your word. Have nothing else to do with him.

Healthy communication is key to strengthening any relationship, even one with a Bird Man. My biggest concern, though, is that the woman in a relationship with a Bird Man may always have to be the one to insist on open, honest communication. So, keep that in mind should you choose to keep the Bird Man in your life.

My final perspective on communication and the Bird Man is that communication thrives on love and respect, both of which are akin to honesty. Be transparent about your needs, and, yes, insist that he be the same. And when he is, be sure to show empathy and understanding when he opens up about his weaknesses—everyone has them. I'm my daughter's hero, her very own Superman, but the truth is her daddy's got issues like every man on Earth. And I don't know any man who can be a Superman all the time. Your words of affirmation and understanding can be significant in keeping him at home and committed to making your relationship thrive.

Remember, if he opens up, then he's a keeper. But you will need to do so with wisdom and understanding. Otherwise, your Bird Man will fly away.

# WHEN THE GOING GETS TOUGH, THE DOG MAN GETS GOING.

*Keishorne Scott*

*Chapter 6*
# The Dog Man

**Three Views:**

H ere are three scenarios that explain the Dog Man in a nutshell. See if one of them comes close to anything you've ever dealt with or may be dealing with now.

## Scenario One

### *The Skank*

"Don't tell me he left you for that skanky girl?"
"Yeah. I found out after our last argument that he was sleeping around with his big-breasted secretary. I just wish I had known sooner."

"Didn't I tell you about my ex-husband who did the same thing with my best friend? Men are just dogs!"

## Scenario Two

### *The Hoe-Man*

"You won't believe what I heard today!" "What's that?"

"I found out that my gym instructor was sleeping with another student."

"Who? Antoine? Why are you acting so surprised?

He ain't' nothing but a hoe himself."

"Well, his girlfriend is a co-worker. I don't know if I should tell her or not."

"I wouldn't bother if I were you. Don't you know men are dogs?"

**Scenario Three**

*The Active Sports Guy*

"What happened to the guy who plays golf just shows that men are dogs."

"Yeah, I heard he slept with 12 women." "No. It's actually 15."

"Wow. That guy deserves all the public humiliation that happens to him. I can't imagine what his wife is going through."

## All Men Are Dogs

We've all heard this one too many times, and there may be a relatively high degree of certainty that you believe this saying too. And why is that? Because you may have had a guy, or two, in your life who was unfaithful to you for no good reason. After that, you made up your mind that all men are dogs. This belief is probably the only thing about men that women around the world, irrespective of race, education, and upbringing, tend to agree upon. It's no wonder that this factoid among hurt women across the world is probably the most used line when it comes to defining relationships. That is the man in the relationship is a dog. Nothing less. But is this the true nature of all men? Are all of us dogs?

Before you jump to conclusions, read through the descriptions and explanation I give on what makes some men the Dog Man. Why is your man behaving the way he does? How can you help prevent him from straying? As you are reading, notice if you can draw any parallels between the Dog Man and your man. The following bit of information might be just what you need.

### Loyalty

It is often said that a dog is a man's best friend, and rightfully so. I believe that at some time in their life, everyone should experience the joy of owning a dog. Not only do dogs possess all of the qualities we look for in a companion, but they also lack those qualities and habits that we often find irritating when it comes to our friends and family. For example, upon returning home from a hard day's work, the owner is cheerfully greeted by her dog. It's as though his yelps say one thing: "I am so happy you are back. Just your being here makes me happy." From my own experience, I find that dogs are loyal, caring, and enthusiastic. They are not offended easily, rude or mean as people can often be. But when it comes to the Dog Man, is he really your best friend?

If you are in a relationship with the kind of guy who will go to hell and back to do all your bidding, make you feel safe and protected, and will tear down the walls of Jericho to make sure you have your way, then you are dancing with the Dog Man. The Dog Man is that kind of man who will get into a fight he knows he is going to lose just to save your honor. Say, for instance, you are at dinner with your man and a rude guy steps on your foot without a snippet of an apology. If you're with a Dog Man, he will make a scene out of it, attempt to beat the offending guy (or receive a beat down, whatever works) to make a statement that no one messes with you and gets away with it. He is fiercely loyal and protective. Dogs often put themselves in harm's way so that you can be safe. They will bark and stand guard at your door to prevent the entry of an intruder. Is the man taking up your time anything like this?

The Dog Man will offer to chaperone you sometimes. For example, if you have a night out with friends, because he's worried that about your safety he will offer to come along. If you get caught at the mall in the middle of a blizzard (blizzards happen a lot where I reside), the Dog Man is going to come there to pick you up. He is that caring and loyal.

Dogs are always willing to go on an adventure with you, whether it is going to the park for a day or something as simple as walking with you down the driveway to get your mail out of the mailbox. In fact, in many instances I find that my dog gives me a reason to get out of the house, thus motivating me to work out. They are always more than happy to tag along with you, making your chores and daily outings a little pleasanter. Similarly, the Dog Man wants to be with you every step of the way. He's just that kind of man. He will be there for you, providing you with moral support, even if he doesn't fully understand the details of whatever it is you are doing in life—whether it's completing a work-related project or making a career change. This brings me to this point about men in general when it comes to relationships; for any relationship to grow and thrive there must be a satisfactory level of care, loyalty, and protection. A woman should feel protected in the arms of the person she loves. A man should always be able to stand up for his woman whenever the occasion demands it.

## Listener

When you're sad, there's no one better to lie with you while you cry. A dog will offer his ears and presence without interrupting or giving his unsolicited opinions about the issue. In fact, a dog will listen to you for hours on end without a single argument or complaint.

While it is often true that women are more verbally expressive with their thoughts and so tend to talk more, a man should still be able to provide a listening ear especially when the subject of discussion is an important one. The Dog Man has no issues with this. He lives for you. The ability to listen without interrupting or judging is essential, and the Dog Man is one of those men who can listen without judging. The Dog Man can provide a listening ear without giving feedback unless when prompted. Sometimes, despondent women aren't even looking for feedback. They want a listening ear.

## Protector

Generally speaking, a dog keeps watch over his master's house. He will not allow anyone to touch anything belonging to his master, and that dog will bark come hell or high water to scare the life out of a stranger who gets too close to his master's house.

In much the same way as a dog keeps watch over his master's house, the Dog Man will go to any length to protect you physically, financially or otherwise. As his companion, you will find that he is capable of providing some detectable level of security in the relationship. These actions don't always translate to having to have massive biceps. But if that helps scare off danger, then that's awesome.

## True Companion

Whenever I'm having a rough day, nothing lifts my spirits more than walking through my front door and seeing my dog sitting up and waiting patiently for me. I don't know of anyone else who is more excited to see me every day than he is. With the anticipation I can see in his eyes when he sees me, it is an instant self-esteem boost to know that someone missed me so much while I was gone.

The sheer excitement in his eyes when he sees me opening the front door is enough to brighten even my darkest moods. I find that dogs are the most loyal and patient companions a person could ever have. The Dog Man can also be boisterous or calm when the situation calls for either. And you want to be with him because he is also someone who knows how to brighten your day.

We all need someone to miss us when we are not around. So why in the world should we be content in a relationship where our absence isn't felt? When I was younger, I would go over to my neighbor's house to swim in the pool in his backyard. While doing laps in his pool, my dog Candy would sit patiently in the front yard for hours waiting for me to come home. I never had to worry about her running away; she would quietly lie in the grass beneath a tree and wait until I was done. She didn't fret or whine while I was away. Candy knew that she and I were companions, and, as such, I would return home to her. She knew that it would only be a matter of time before I gave her my undivided attention again. In the case of the Dog Man, I believe he is that kind of man who will yearn for your attention and doesn't mind waiting to get it.

There is pure bliss in having your man drive to your workplace to pick you up after a long day at work. The Dog Man is that kind of man who desires your attention and loves to reciprocate.

There are even times when he doesn't mind waiting to get in some one-on-one time with you.

## Helper

Dogs are beneficial animals. Some can sense when their owner is sick. Others, acting as a guide, help their blind masters cross the street safely. It's as though they welcome a relationship or partnership with their master that is mutually beneficial. The master cuddles with his companion, making sure he's always taken care of and, in turn, his helpful dog fetches for this or that at a moment's command. And, as I said before, the beloved pet will even guard the home as best he can. Again, both the owner and the dog get something out of the relationship.

Since this chapter is about the Dog Man and his woman, what exactly is that partnership like between the two of them? Is it anything like that of a dog and his owner? In simple terms, here's my take on the Dog Man's ability to fulfill a partnership that is mutually beneficial. It's not that he can't. It's about his willingness to do so. After all, there is no point being in a relationship if both partners are not helpful to each other. So here are some questions I believe you should consider if you are in a relationship with the Dog Man and are thinking of marriage. When the two of you discuss money, does he speak of sacrificing a part (or all) of his earnings to help you out of a financial mess (if you are in one)?

Don't get me wrong. It is not his responsibility to get you out of anything, and vice versa. However, the two of you must be realistic. Any binds you're in you're going to need each other's help getting out, should you decide to marry. Therefore, if your Dog Man leans towards self-centeredness, you're out of luck. There will be no sacrifices, no considerations of your present situation, no genuine desire to help you out of anything.

Contrarily, some of you may be dating a Dog Man who is the kind of man who uses everything at his disposal to help you. If that is the case, he will discuss spending a future with you (i.e., marriage) where he plans on things like putting his assets up for sale to raise money to help fulfill your dreams and needs. The Dog Man recognizes an advantage of there being a fusion of funds to keep the partnership healthy and thriving.

Here's the bottom line on the Dog Man when it comes to helping you: Any time a man sacrifices for your benefit and welfare he exhibits the helping trait of the Dog Man, in which case you should not be surprised about his selfless acts, like showing up at your place with paint rollers and design magazines in hand to help you with the décor even though he could have just called to check on your progress in decorating your home. Or maybe he'll show up with dinner after you've had a long day and are too tired to fix yourself something.

## *Chapter 7*

# The Dark Side of the Dog Man

Ask women on any given day to describe men in one word, and nearly all of them will give the same response: dogs. Without even pausing to think, these women quickly sum up all men as dogs. It's not a sexist comment, in my opinion; it's simply how a lot of women feel about most men. Because I have advised on relationships for some time now, I do not fully agree with that staple sentiment. In my time as a relationship coach, I've seen plenty of men step up to the plate as accountable, caring fathers and husbands. So, for me, this sentiment is a non-fact. At the same time, I am a realist who has witnessed members of my gender treat women poorly and laugh it off as nothing, in which case I understand women's frustration behind the characterization of men. That's why I wrote this additional chapter on the Dog Man. These similarities, ladies, should not be ignored or set aside as trivial during the dating stage; doing so will mean enduring needless hurt and putting up with a courtship dogged by one disappointment after another. With that said, I want to make a case for avoiding the Dog Man. He's a dangerous, thoughtless man who will piss all over your happiness.

In the previous chapter, I drew a comparison between men and dogs. Since we tend to think of dogs as loyal companions, loyal protectors, and loyal family members, it's natural to think of men that way, given the similarities between the two. However, the comparison is only superficial at best, as you'll soon see, making that sentiment you read earlier about many members of my gender spot-on. Way too many of us men can be dogs in the worst sense of that label. And, I might add, many of us of know it and are not about to change—which is why women need to be extremely careful to examine every man who comes sniffing around her before she even thinks about calling him "the one". Here are some ways in which the two are alike. By no means are these similarities drawn from rocket science. I realize there are definite differences between men and dogs. I could not help noticing that what may be negative characteristics of dogs also exist in some men. It's these men you should avoid at all cost.

## Unreasonable Jealousy

At times you may notice that your dog may be distant, acting like it doesn't care about you and what you do until another dog enters the house and you start giving the visiting dog all the attention. The visiting dog wags his tail in joyfulness to be in your presence, while your dog becomes jealous and begins to do little tricks to set your attention on him. Frankly, he'll probably make a nuisance of himself while showing off to get your attention.

In similar fashion to the show-off, most men become jealous when other men get close to the woman they're pursuing. Though this is understandable and expected, the Dog Man's jealousy can be a little over the top. Let's say you have a friend by the name of Sam who calls you often—in one day. To ease your Dog Man, you pretty much have to be quick to explain that those calls are from Samantha instead of Samuel. Admittedly, spending an hour or more on the phone with your girlfriend might even raise his quizzical eyebrows.

My editor shared this story with me about one of her sisters who was once married to the Dog Man. Her sister—an extrovert who loves people—would spend considerable time chatting with her girlfriends over the phone. Being the dog that this former husband was at the time, he accused his dear wife of being a lesbian. Yes, this idiot of a dog was so jealous that his wife—who also happened to be beautiful— spent time talking to people other than himself. Over time, their marriage disintegrated, and The Dog Man married another woman who fell under the same cruel accusations. That is just how jealous this one Dog Man became when his wives gave others some attention. By the way, this Dog Man's second marriage ended in divorce as well. In case you're wondering, my editor tells me he's on to his third marriage. I feel sorry for his poor, misguided third trial— um, I mean wife.

One more thing about the out-of-control jealousy, though I think a more fitting word for it is territorial. Like a dog in real life, the Dog Man marks his territory—in this case you—and proceeds to prevent intruders from wandering in. Now, while that may seem harmless on the one hand (that he'd protect you), it may spell danger on the other. Case in point: if another man looks at his woman, the dog in him emerges, and a brutal physical fight looms in the distance. If your man's anger is rage—whether it's directed at you or someone else—you may have a Dog Man on your hands. And that is not cool. He is likely incapable of controlling his aggression, which means his woman will not do a better job of managing it either. I would like to think no woman wants a man who cannot properly guard his emotions. And if you are in a relationship right now with a man whose emotions get out of control, leave that man. His uncontrollable aggression will eventually turn on you and put your very life in danger. You're worth more than that, and there is so much in life stored up for your greatness. So, leave that Dog Man or kick him out, and live your life free of physical abuse.

## The Strayer

A dog can love his master and be the most loyal, compassionate creature. Nonetheless, some of these very loving creatures develop a reputation of straying into the waiting arms of another owner. This may happen because they are given the opportunity to do what they love best—explore their environment freely, without a leash, or are told how far they might wander (i.e., stray away from their owner). As I said, dogs love exploring and often misbehave when given too much freedom. They become very promiscuous in that they mate (or attempt to) with just about every eligible bitch in sight, knocking a few up along the way. Thus, the uncanny similarity the straying dog has in common with the human Dog Man. For the Dog Man, freedom does not always play well in his favor. The dog in that man still finds a way out when presented the opportunity.

Now, I have often overheard other women fault the Dog Man's tendency to stray into the arms of another. The woman will be accused of not giving him enough sex and attention. Granted, the Dog Man's woman may be able to prevent his cheating— if she had a leash on him the whole time! But how ridiculous and immature is that? It's insane! What grown, strong, intelligent woman wants to be stuck with leashing a man to keep him in control and underfoot? Besides, if he were a real man at all, he would know that accountability is key to maintaining and growing a relationship. Otherwise, what's the use? Further, I do not believe that it's either partner's responsibility to hold the other in check. You're both grown. You're each responsible for what you do and for correcting your flaws.

## The Bottom Line with the Dog Man

Dogs are cute, adorable and loving even. In fact, their cuteness makes you want to cuddle with them all day and keep them around for life. Their antics will keep you laughing and feeling good that you have one. And, yes, they can be loyal and great at keeping danger at bay, which may be the best thing about them.

But here's the thing; when it comes to a man, having these characteristics is not that cute. In fact, a woman needs to be careful falling for a man who is so territorial that he suspects her of cheating on him at every turn. And speaking of having a cheating spirit—the Dog Man is prime for wandering in another's territory and sticking his nozzle where he shouldn't. I mention all this to say, as loyal as he can sometimes be, it is my opinion as a man that no woman should ever hook up with something that resembles the Dog Man as I have described him in this book.

If you find yourself somehow in love with the likes of the Dog Man, I have an easy one-word solution that can be easily implemented: leave.

# I LEAD, I PROTECT, I COMFORT, I LOVE, I ENCOURAGE. THERE IS NO MAN EQUAL TO ME. LOOK NO FURTHER. I AM YOUR LION MAN.

# Chapter *8*
## The Lion Man

Admit it. If there wasn't another chapter to read, you would have settled for the Dog Man, declared this was the best you could do, put a leash around him to keep him out of trouble and consider yourself "lucky" to have such a good doggie-man. Right? Well, that's not the best you can do, as you will see a little later; you're not lucky if you have someone like him as a companion. Besides, if you have to leash a grown man to make him behave, that makes you a pet owner not a girlfriend or a wife.

You may think that, because I'm a man, I would only see things from a man's point of view and do what I could to convince you that men are not dogs, birds or mice. But as a man who cares about the future choice of my daughter, let me be the first to say it—some men are nothing more than a dog, a bird or a mouse. I will do everything in my power to help my daughter understand that yearning for anything less than what she deserves is the same as settling. She was not created to settle for K9s when it comes to her destiny and neither were you. Her mother and I will teach her that there are people who were specifically born for her life and vice versa. Therefore, she will miss out on the best if she settles for the least. She is a queen. You are a queen. And queens marry kings not dogs, birds or mice.

This chapter is a little different from the previous ones because it is mostly a teaching chapter. There will be times when I will ask thought-provoking questions to help you understand and strongly consider the Lion Man instead of the Dog Man, the Bird Man or the Mouse Man.

What I consider the second half of this chapter is getting you ready for your king. Every queen goes through a season when she must do certain things in preparation for the day she meets her king. Yours is no different. For example, there will be times when I will have you do a deeper dive into your psyche to understand your 'why' (which I will explain later), which gets you ready for life with your Lion Man. Incidentally, this deeper dive is also facilitating your being able to carry the 'weight' of being with a king. That's right. Kings bear a heavy weight, and I don't mean a physical weight. Their weight is in the strength of their personality, which will be illustrated in the next section. The thing is you need to prepare for that weight so that it doesn't overwhelm you. Lastly, the second half of this chapter is a look at how you can position yourself for the Lion Man. Positioning is important and should not be sidestepped. It's one of those things that prepare you for the man who is meant for you. So, before we get into any of that, let me explain the nature of the lion.

## PART I

## The Lion and the Lion Man

### The Lion

There's a reason why the God I worship calls Himself a "lion", and because He made me in His own likeness, He considers me to be one as well. But what does it mean to be a lion? Does it mean I'm loud? Mean? Scary? Hairy? To find the answer, I did some research on lions. I figured if I'm considered one, I may as well understand what comes with that metaphor. Here's what I discovered from my readings on this prodigious "king of the beasts".

The lion symbolizes strength and authority. This terror of the forest can successfully prey upon and carry away something as large as a horse, bull or elephant! To be endowed with that much power and strength is mind-boggling, not to mention dauntless and bold.

During my research, I was also impressed with his presence of command and authority, as evidenced by his roar, which can be heard miles away. It's a deafening, frightening deep sound that alerts nearby prey that resistance is futile and their death is imminent. No wonder animals within earshot of the king's roar flee the area to safer ground as quickly as their four legs will take them.

The leadership of this terror of the forests is as striking as his stealthy, controlled walk through his kingdom. He's never in much of a hurry unless his prey is trying to get away from him. As I said before, the lion has this roar that makes anybody take notice. Take the female lion, for instance; she makes sure she forms a pride, which comes in handy with the caretaking of her cubs. A pride of lions takes care of one another's family. For instance, when one of them is away, the others take over, looking after her young until she returns, which means the pride provides instant, available protection. Now, that's leadership.

## The Lion Man

Undeniably, we men could learn a lesson or two from the characteristics of the lion. But since I wrote this book to help women be on the lookout for a suitable partner, I want to turn my attention to what she needs to look for in the Lion Man—a man I believe every woman deserves. Nothing less.

Let me begin with leadership. Based on what we have seen in the mouse, the bird, and the dog, this might be the hardest trait to live by. But for the Lion Man, leading is second nature. You may have gotten a sense of what leadership looks like among lions; well, here is leadership applied to men. A man who leads does not leave his family in danger when he is away. He secures the premises with either electronic security or having other family and friends stop by to make sure you are okay. In fact, your safety is his number one priority at all times. There is no level of need concerning you where the Lion Man will not take leadership, and this includes the provision. In the forest of the lions, not even the cubs want for food.

It's the same leadership principle applied to the Lion Man. Like the pride, he sees to it that your physical needs are taken care of as well as the children's. That means you do not have to beg him over and over to leave you money for food, gas, entertainment or even to join you in the financial planning of your future together, and so on. Leaders do not have to be poked, prodded and threatened to do what is right; they just do it. From my own experience and from observing other strong men who have been in my life, I can honestly say that the Lion Man is a leader, and he's got your back.

I mentioned earlier that the lion has incredible physical strength. He's so strong that his power can even overwhelm a full-size elephant. Well, maybe the Lion Man may not be muscular with the physical strength of a bodybuilder, but he has a sharp mind that challenges other men. For example, the Lion Man believes he is capable of doing all things and doing all things well. Further, he believes the same about you, without thinking of you as competition. For a lot of men, that is not the case. A woman who earns more, for example, is competition. Consequently, insecurity sets in and intrudes upon the relationship in the form of petty arguments, jealousy over the woman's promotions, bonuses, and attention from others because of her success. On and on it goes.

Another strength of the Lion Man is that he does not have a problem with encouraging you or anyone else. In fact, he's so secure in himself that he does not have a problem helping you to be the best version of yourself. Again, competition with you is not his thing. He wants you to be successful—not because it brings more income in the home or prestige to your relationship but because he believes success is your destiny. You're the head, not the tail. You are above, not beneath him or anyone else.

Here is something else you can rest assured you will find in a Lion Man—his loyalty. Unlike the Mouse Man, the Bird Man or the Dog Man, the Lion Man is a committed, one-woman man. Whereas the other men described in this book look for ways to get out of a relationship with you, the Lion Man looks for ways to grow his relationship with you. He does not want out. He wants in—all the time. So, do not be surprised if he is the one to suggest that the two of you join a club for married couples where there are plenty of teachings on how to strengthen your relationship. He will be all in when it comes to going on trips with other couples as a way to relax and learn the principles of doing marriage well.

As I said, this man plans to stay with you for life and will do whatever it takes to make it happen. By the way, the leader in him seeks to identify ways to strengthen a good thing, and he thinks life with you is a good thing. You need not worry about the Lion Man taking flight, like a Bird Man you may have dated in the past. On the contrary, the Lion Man fights for what he loves. And he will always look for ways to show that you are loved.

## Part II

### Getting Ready for Your Lion Man

Before my wife and I got married, we knew wholeheartedly that we had to be ready for marriage. Marriage itself carries such a weight that if you are not prepared for it, it will crush you. I am not talking about the wedding day, which, compared to a lifetime of being with the same person, is a walk in the park. There are preparations and a state of readiness to bring someone into your life. If you are not properly prepared to be married, then married life will prove difficult for you, even if you somehow wind up with the Lion Man.

Because I have seen so many of my female friends and female relatives enter marriage without really being prepared, I wrote the following sections to help you steer clear of the failures they encountered all because they were not prepared. Mind you, they wanted the very best—like a Lion Man to be married to—even though they were not prepared to step into a relationship, which brings me to this question: If I had not described the Lion Man to you, would you be able to recognize such a king? Even if your answer is, "Yes," read on. I think the information you will gather from the next section may surprise you, for I doubt you have thought about a lot of the things I raise.

# How Will I Recognize My King?

His purpose or destiny has a definite place in your life, so definite, in fact, that it will align with your own. That's why you should marry for tomorrow, not today. What do I mean by this? I believe your king was born for you, and you were born just for him. It is purpose that will eventually bring you two together, and it is purpose that will keep you together in a fulfilled relationship. And notice I said purpose would maintain your relationship, not love. Love is great. Love is sweet. Love is kind. But it is also here today and gone tomorrow. When storms of disagreements come—and they will come—feelings and emotions seesaw, but the purpose for the two of you coming together in the first place and wanting to be together forever stays the same.

Here's the thing; way too many people do not know their purpose or destiny because they lack vision for their lives. It is the vision that shapes a person's future, and destiny drives your decisions, including whom to date. Sure, people do stuff and are sometimes very successful at it, but that doesn't mean what they do day in and day out is for them to do. If this is you, then know that you are wasting your days, and time is way too precious to waste on anyone and anything. So you must have a vision for life in order to know your purpose. Otherwise, without a clear-cut vision that gives way to purpose, you will risk settling for the dog, the bird or, worse yet, the mouse.

In other words, you will miss the lion that was destined for you because your lack of purpose led you into certain settings and situations where the mouse, the bird or the dog thrives. But purpose-driven Lion Men avoid these same areas because their vision calls for something better, more significant and challenging. They know they are made for something greater than themselves, so the non-challenging environments and careers and so on that attract the mouse, the bird, and the dog will not work for the lion. He wants something greater, and he's going after it. And strong-minded lions go where they are called.

Now that I have established that purpose should be the driving force behind a relationship, naturally you're thinking, *Okay, so how do I find my purpose?*

*How do I know what I'm doing is what I was meant to do? How do I know I am where I am supposed to be?* Simple. You ask. It's what my wife and I did when we were single. In our case, we asked God to show us His vision for our lives, including what a healthy marriage would look like. We believed He held the blueprint for our lives since He says He's the One who had already written the vision (Jeremiah 29:11).

Once we tapped into His vision, we were able to identify our purpose. Since we believe that He is the One who created us, we went straight to the Creator. We point-blank asked God, "Why did You make me? Why was I thought in Your head in the first place? What exactly did You make me to do?" The whole point is you are not an accident. Nobody is. So, seek to understand your 'why' for being here right now. As I mentioned, my wife and I consulted our God for counsel. You may wish to use some other measurement to help you discover your purpose.

As a life coach, I strongly recommend you find focus in this area before you seek to be found by your king. Rest assured, he's out there, but it is in your best interest that you find you first before you seek to be found by someone else. Otherwise, you risk transforming yourself into someone you are not just to be with a man. And women who live outside of purpose typically wind up with anything but a lion king. Here's another reason to know your 'why'. In reality, lions do things with purpose, their day-to-day actions are not ambiguous. They always have a plan for something. For example, they purpose to travel in a pack (tribe) to stave off potential attacks from other animals. They are not just hanging around together to be cool. They know their purpose and fulfill it. Similarly, I believe every Lion Man is attracted to and wants a woman who knows her 'why'. In fact, during the dating period, a Lion Man's favorite kind of question is almost always related to why.

Look for him to ask the same kinds of questions my wife and I had to ask God, just to be clear about our future together. Now, he may not exactly start the question with the word why, but listen carefully; he's still interviewing you for your 'why'. For example, his 'why' question may be more like "Do you enjoy doing what you do?" Don't be thrown off. It's still a 'why' question. Translated into Lion Man language, that question is asking, "Why do you do what you do?" Here's another 'why' question a Lion Man may ask: "What's your purpose for being?"

Plain and simple, the Lion Man wants to know "Why do you think you're here?" And, ladies, one more thing; you need to be asking these same 'why' questions of the men you date. Remember dating without purpose is a waste of your time.

## How Do I Find My King?

You don't. Men do the hunting. I believe it is not your responsibility, not your destiny, not your reason for being to hunt your king out. That is so important that I need to repeat it, so let me. Despite the high intelligence women no doubt possess, I do not believe they were intended to be the hunters of men. Sure, you inspect men upon meeting them to check their suitability for you. That's fine and is what you are supposed to do. But hunting them? No, it's a king's responsibility to look for his queen. The man for your purpose should be on the hunt for you.

Now, as you rest in that, I want you to think about something else. Are you in a position to be found by your heaven-sent king? The question is simple enough, but are you ready for the answer? If so, keep reading.

# How Should I be Positioned to be Found?

Ladies, positioning is extremely important. It is so important that many people miss out on their purpose because they were not in a position to take it in the first place. Your Lion Man is a part of your purpose. However, he will not find you until you are in a position to be found.

So, what do I mean by positioning yourself? It's this simple: Positioning begins with under-standing anything and everything about yourself, including your likes, your dislikes, your propensi-ties, your strengths, your weaknesses, your fears, what makes you laugh, what makes you cry, what your non-negotiables are, and so on. In case you're wondering what knowing yourself inside out has to do with relationships, I'll give it to you straight, no chaser. What you are you attract.

If you are anything like a mouse, a bird or a dog yourself, then that is the kind of man who will always engineer his way into your life. Lowlives are geniuses at attracting women who have no idea who they really are. You're a queen, girl —that's who you are— and you were made by Royal Hands, destined for a king. But if you do not begin to understand this, you will operate outside your royal DNA and continue to attract lowlives. And lowlives do not honor queens because they don't know how.

Here's the thing; if you do not like what you generally attract, then you need to seriously think about why you attract a particular type of man over and over, only to get hurt over and over again. I'm not saying every woman in the world needs to undergo some sort of change, but I am suggesting that if you want the outlook on your relationship with men to change, you may want to examine the whys and wherefores of you before you date another man. Seriously. Think about this; there may be some things in your becoming that don't need to have a place in your life at all.

If you're not sure what those things are, then ask your BFF, a family member or even an associate what changes she thinks you should consider making to become a stronger, better you. The revelations may be the thing you need to hear. And, if you agree and make those changes, I have a feeling you will begin to attract a different kind of man, like the Lion Man you deserve.

There are some other things you can do to position yourself to be found by your Lion Man. I admit these suggestions may not be for every woman, but I think they will help keep every woman out of a wasteland of hurt and humiliation that comes from being found by the wrong one.

## Being in Position to be Found

You have to position yourself mentally. About a page or so ago, I asked you to think about a few things you may do that are causing you to attract the wrong men. Now I want you to think about what you think of yourself. For example, do you think of yourself as a queen? I don't mean now and then or on special occasions but every day. How often do you think of yourself as a woman who deserves the royal treatment that is sincere and from the heart? For some women, this sounds like a stupid question because they may be thinking, *Who wouldn't think she's good enough for a king? Plenty*! Based on some people I grew up with, went to high school with, and even dated before I married. They were women who were no stranger to being abused, cheated on, assaulted or humiliated all the time by men. They would date the mouse, the bird or the dog because they didn't think they were worth anything beyond those animals.

Their mindset about who they were and who they could become needed repositioning. If this is you, I want you to think about something. Your mind is your greatest asset, not your gender, your butt, your breasts, your gorgeous legs or ability to love or even have sex. Your greatest, strongest asset is your mind. But, believe it or not, this precious asset can also be your greatest enemy. You read right. Your brain is not your friend. It will run crazy with thoughts that are negative and detrimental to you unless you discipline it otherwise.

Here is something I do every day to teach my mind: I speak affirmations over my life, my health, my home and family, my business, my speaking engagements, my abilities and so on.

I do not leave my mindset to random thinking. My thoughts are purposeful just like my very life.

The end goal for me is to think positively of myself, beginning with the notion that I deserve to be treated with respect by everyone I meet. I don't have a lot of space in this book to teach you other things to do to tame your mindset, but if you begin with practicing affirmations over yourself, you are on your way to positioning yourself to be found by your king.

Mentally positioning yourself is a good start, but it's not enough. You need to physically position yourself to be found by the right man. You have to do something! Get involved with a cause, for example. Find a community outreach program or project that you can be of assistance to. Have a passion for something beyond you. You would be surprised at how many 'lions' are involved with worthy causes. In fact, it's the nature of lions to be passionate about something and go after it. Lion Men are the same way with a cause.

Here's some straight talk on the physicality of being found: If you want to stop attracting trash, then stop going where trash is. Think about all the places where you met the mouse, the bird or the dog you eventually dated. However, if you met one of these guys at a church, don't stop going to church, but stop being naïve about churchgoing mice, birds, and dogs. They quote Scripture, sing hymns, pray (a little), and still choose to remain perfect counterfeits of what's real. That's why you must know the marks of a lion, the only man worth your time.

This last suggestion has to do with current relationships. If you're single (likely you are, if you are reading this book), right now is the best time to do a lot of traveling with your friends. Go on every trip you can with them since you only have to pack for yourself and funding is limited to just you. Enjoy your friends while you can because once your lion king finds you, you will have to shift some of that attention on to him. So, while you can, hang out with your friends!

Being in a position to be found is also a great way to wait for your king. As I said, he will find you. The trick is not allowing yourself to become so wrapped up about being seen that you lose focus on other important things—like family, friends, traveling, serving others, and so on. Your day-to-day goal is not to be found but to enjoy life as you wait to be hunted by your king. He's on the prowl right now, and he will find you.

# *CONCLUSION*

Toxic men are not your destiny, and it's not your purpose to try to 'fix' them either. Spare yourself the trouble and leave that to God, their pastor or their priest. Your future is with a king who knows how to treat you like a queen. Among the four types of men described in this book, the only one that qualifies for that role is the Lion Man. This is the one who's on the hunt for you right now. And he'll find you as long as you're not with some mouse, bird or dog because the lion looks for prey that is not attached. Then, too, the Lion Man is a gentleman and will not make you leave something that's not good for you, even if he knows that man you're with now is beneath you. Good men are like that—they give you space to let you decide what is good for you. They force neither their opinions nor their bodies on you. As I said, they're gentlemen.

As I see it, if you're with anyone other than a Lion Man, you have a decision to make. You must detach and detox. That's right. Unplug yourself from his life as quickly as you can. If you take a minute and think about how the mouse, bird or dog makes you feel, you will probably admit this man does not energize you to be a better person or grow in your purpose. In fact, most of the time, you're discontent just being around him. Toxic men do that, you know—they suck the life right out of you because their focus is on themselves. It's no wonder just about all their efforts go into getting others to serve them, instead of the other way around. If you recall, I never made any illusions about generosity with these guys. They're not generous. Like the lion, they carefully seek out their prey. However, unlike the Lion

Man, they are not into reciprocating love the way God wanted you to be loved.

Now, if you are in a relationship with a mouse, a bird or a dog, detaching yourself from him is not all it takes to leave him in your past. You've got to detox from him as well. For starters, leave. If you're already married to any of these toxic men, I suggest counseling with a professional or your priest or pastor. Then forgive him for being everything he isn't and wasn't with you. As long as you hang on to ill feelings, he has the upper hand on your emotions and gets to control what you think about all other men. Detoxing from this man keeps his name off your lips and stinging memories of him out of your thought life. Otherwise, the topic of your conversations will almost always be about him. Besides, no man wants to be with a woman who's forever recalling the other guy. I can't put this simpler. Your Lion Man is looking for you and will miss you if you are attached to another man—physically and emotionally. So, forgive and move on.

And don't forget this nugget: Compatibility and love are not all it takes to make a marriage. Purpose must connect you and your future spouse. In fact, God's purpose will be the driving force that keeps you and your Mr. Right together. Do not be tempted into dropping God's purpose as a priority when choosing your spouse. Anything else won't do!

You have an abundant, full life ahead of you if you actively and intentionally make the right choices when choosing your spouse.

# ACKNOWLEDGMENTS

A million thanks to God for always coming through for me; to my lovely wife, Princess, for showing me unconditional love and adding to my story every day; and to my amazing editor, Yvonne Perry, who made writing this book a little bit easier.

# ABOUT THE AUTHOR

Keishorne Scott is a Man of God, husband, great father, relationship coach, bestselling author and renowned speaker. He currently resides in New York with his family.

If you would like to bring Keishorne's unique empowerment message to your social or faith-based setting, contact his team at www.keishornescott. com. Or you may write Keishorne at info@ keishornescott.com.

•RESOURCES

FOLLOW KEISHORNE
Website: www.keishornescott.com

 @keishornescott
@KeishorneScott

# APPENDIX

(Relationship Surveys)

# *Get It Right Now*

Choosing a spouse is the most significant decision you will ever make. There are so many factors to consider and weigh, not to mention those discussed earlier. I think it comes down to asking the right questions of yourself and your potential spouse for life. So, why take chances and get it wrong? To keep you out of divorce court, I have put together a list of websites that offer a checklist of all the right questions to ask and things to do before you tell anybody, "I do." And one last suggestion; to check for similarities between you and him, get your potential partner to read the same articles and follow through with the same instructions. If he resists, drop him. You don't have time to play games or to coax him into anything.

"Dating Checklist: When You Start a New Relationship" by Seth Meyers, Psy.D.

https://www.psychologytoday.com/blog/ insight-is-2020/201207/dating-checklist-when-you-start-new-relationship

"10 Questions for Choosing Ms. or Mr. Right"

https://www.meetmindful.com/articles-dating-10-questions-for-choosing-ms-or-mr-right/

"How to identify behaviors that undermine love—and how to avoid drifting apart" by Randi Gunther, Ph.D.

https://www.psychologytoday.com/blog/ redis-covering-love/201412/ten-important- questions-you-should-ask-potential-partner

"Sailing Happily Ever After"

http://www.sailinghappilyeverafter.com/ relation-ship-assessment-for-couples/t

Made in the USA
Lexington, KY
20 May 2019